FARMSTAND FAVORITES

Pumpkins

Over 75 Farm Fresh Recipes

D1525721

Farmstand Favorites: Pumpkins
Text copyright © 2010 Hatherleigh Press

Hatherleigh Press is committed to preserving and protecting the natural resources of the Earth. Environmentally responsible and sustainable practices are embraced within the company's mission statement.

Hatherleigh Press is a member of the Publishers Earth Alliance, committed to preserving and protecting the natural resources of the planet while developing a sustainable business model for the book publishing industry.

This book was edited and designed in the village of Hobart, New York. Hobart is a community that has embraced books and publishing as a component of its livelihood. There are several unique bookstores in the village. For more information, please visit www.hobartbookvillage.com.

www.hatherleighpress.com

DISCLAIMER
This book offers general cooking and eating suggestions for educational purposes only. In no case should it be a substitute nor replace a healthcare professional. Consult your healthcare professional to determine which foods are safe for you and to establish the right diet for your personal nutritional needs.

Library of Congress Cataloging-in-Publication Data

Pumpkins : over 75 farm-fresh recipes.
    p. cm. -- (Farmstand favorites)
  ISBN 978-1-57826-357-8 (pbk. : alk. paper) 1. Cooking (Pumpkin) I. Hatherleigh Press.
  TX803.P93P866 2010
  641.6'562--dc22
                        2010030112

All Hatherleigh Press titles are available for bulk purchase, special promotions, and premiums. For information about reselling and special purchase opportunities, please call 1-800-528-2550 and ask for the Special Sales Manager.

Cover Design by Nick Macagnone
Interior Design by Nick Macagnone
Photography by Catarina Astrom

10 9 8 7 6 5 4 3 2 1

Table of Contents

All About Pumpkins

Pumpkins, and their seeds, are rich in both nutritional and medicinal benefits. Centuries ago, Native Americans recognized the many uses for this member of the *Cucurbita* family, which also includes squash, watermelon, and cucumbers, and included them as a staple in their diets. The early settlers and explorers later incorporated them into their eating regimen as well, and carried the seeds with them when they returned to Europe, further spreading the cultivation and popularity of pumpkins. Today, over 1.5 billion pounds of pumpkins are produced annually in the United States, making it one of the world's leading pumpkin producers. Other top world producers include Mexico, India, and China.

Health Benefits of Pumpkins

Pumpkins are packed full of beneficial vitamins, minerals, and nutrients. They are high in vitamins A, C, K, and E. They contain high levels of alpha and beta-carotene, antioxidant carotenoids, fiber, water, and essential minerals like zinc, iron, magnesium, and potassium. The fruit of the pumpkin also serves as a natural laxative.

The seeds, oil, and juice from pumpkins have many health and nutritional properties as well. Pumpkin seeds are used to promote prostate and kidney health, control cholesterol levels, and aid in anti-inflammatory treatment for arthritis. Pumpkin oil, taken from the seeds, is also helpful in reducing cholesterol. Even the juice from the pumpkin can be drank

Did you know?

- The largest pumpkin recorded weighed in at 1,725 pounds. Christy Harp became the current Guinness World Record champion for growing it on October 3, 2009.

- America's top pumpkin-producing states are Pennsylvania, Ohio, California and Illinois.

and aids with ulcers and high acidity problems. Essentially every part of the pumpkin contains health and healing properties, making it a wise addition to any diet.

There are hundreds of varieties of pumpkins. They all fall in one of these four groups:

Cucurbita Moschata – These pumpkins usually have a tan-colored skin. They are often used for commercially canned pumpkins.

Cucurbita Pepo – Members in this group are generally the ones used for Jack-o-Lanterns and carving. They also include miniature varieties.

Cucurbita Mixta – Pumpkins in this group usually have a white, cream, green, or striped skin.

Cucurbita Maxima – Members of this group are the giant pumpkins.

Below are a few tips to remember when selecting the best pumpkins:

- Choose pumpkins with stems intact. Ones without stems will not last as long.
- Avoid ones with soft spots, holes, cuts in the skin, or bruises.
- Select a pumpkin with a hard rind and free from discoloration.
- Never carry the pumpkin by the stem. They detach easily and will then make that area of the pumpkin more susceptible to rot.

Proper storage will ensure the longevity and optimize the taste and freshness of your pumpkins. Follow these simple steps:

- Store pumpkins in a cool, dry location.

Did you know?

- At one time, pumpkins were believed to cure snake bites and remove freckles.
- Pumpkin pie originated from American colonists who would cut off the top of the pumpkin and gut it; add milk, spices, and honey; and then bake it. The pumpkin shell was the crust!
- Pumpkins can come in almost any color, including blue and red.
- Pumpkin is an ingredient in many anti-wrinkle creams and facial treatments.
- Pumpkins consist of 90% water.

Optimal temperature is 50-55°F with a relative humidity between 50-70%. High humidity will cause an increase in rot and decay. Low humidity will cause the fruit to dry out.

- If you are storing more than one pumpkin, place them in a single layer, allowing space between them.

- Do not store pumpkins near apples. Apples exude ethylene gas while they ripen, which will speed up the ripening process of the pumpkins, making them last for a shorter time.

- Inspect them frequently and remove any pumpkins that are rotting or show signs of damage. Keeping them together will ruin the others.

- Store pumpkin seeds in airtight containers in the refrigerator. They should remain fresh for 1-2 months.

Pumpkins for Beautiful Skin

Harness the many health benefits of pumpkins with these two beauty recipes:

Pumpkin Pie Enzyme Mask
(Courtesy of the National Honey Board)

Ingredients:

3-4 tablespoons ground oats
1 tablespoon milk or heavy cream
2 tablespoons crushed pineapple
¾ cup pumpkin puree, canned or fresh
½ cup honey

Directions:

Mix ground oats and milk or cream in a bowl or mixer. Add crushed pineapple and pumpkin, draining excess water out of fresh pumpkin by squeezing it in a paper towel. Thoroughly blend the ingredients. While stirring, slowly drizzle in the honey, mixing well. Refrigerate in air tight container for 10-14 days. Makes about 4 applications.

To use: Apply liberally with fingertips to face and neck area. Leave mask on for 8-10 minutes. Rinse with warm water and pat dry.

Harvest Pumpkin Exfoliating Mask

(Courtesy of the National Honey Board)

Ingredients:

4 tablespoons pumpkin puree
1 tablespoon honey
4 teaspoons cornmeal
2 teaspoons aloe vera gel
2 teaspoons pineapple, diced
1 teaspoon green tea
½ teaspoon sunflower oil
6 drops frankincense essential oil (optional)
4 drops cinnamon extract (optional)

Directions:

Steep green tea in boiling water. Set aside to cool. In blender or food processor puree pineapple and place in medium-sized mixing bowl. Add pumpkin, honey and aloe. Mix well. Stir in sunflower oil, green tea and cornmeal. Discard the remaining green tea. Add frankincense and cinnamon. Stir. Apply small amount of pumpkin mask to cheeks, forehead, chin and neck. Massage in circular motions gently buffing skin. Repeat. Apply more product as needed. Leave a thin layer of pumpkin mask on face and neck for 15-20 minutes. Rinse with tepid or cool water and pat dry with soft towel. Follow with appropriate moisturizer. Store remaining mask covered in refrigerator for up to 2 weeks. Makes 4 treatments.

Pumpkin enzymes dissolve dead skin cells while the cornmeal sweeps them clean. Honey has antimicrobial properties as well as moisturizes and softens. The result is a beautiful glowing complexion. Use this mask as often as you like.

Breakfast

Pumpkin Mush

Ingredients:
1 pint stewed pumpkin
2 quarts milk
Butter
Corn meal
1 teaspoon ground ginger

Directions:
Pour two quarts or more of milk into a medium saucepan, and
warm. Have ready some pumpkin stewed very soft and dry;
mashed smooth and pressed until all the liquid has drained off.
Then measure a large pint of the stewed pumpkin; mix with it
a piece of fresh butter, and a teaspoon of ground ginger. Stir it
gradually into the milk, as soon as it has come to a boil. Add,
by degrees, a large pint or more of corn meal, a little at a time,
stirring it in. If you find the mush too thin, as you proceed, add
in equal portions, more pumpkin and more meal, until it becomes so thick you can scarcely stir it. After it is all thoroughly
mixed, and has boiled well, reduce heat and allow it to simmer
for about an hour. Eat it warm with butter and molasses, or
with rich milk. It is also very good at lunch in cold weather.

Harvest Pumpkin Muffins
(Courtesy of the National Honey Board)

Ingredients:

1½ cups all-purpose flour
1½ teaspoons baking powder
1 teaspoon baking soda
¼ teaspoon salt
1½ teaspoons ground cinnamon
½ teaspoon ground ginger
¼ teaspoon ground nutmeg

¼ cup (½ stick) butter or margarine, softened
¾ cup honey
1 egg
1 cup solid packed pumpkin
1 cup chopped toasted walnuts

Directions:

In medium bowl, combine flour, baking powder, baking soda, salt, cinnamon, ginger and nutmeg; set aside. Using an electric mixer, beat butter until light; beat in honey, egg and pumpkin. Gradually add flour mixture, mixing until just blended; stir in walnuts. Spoon into 12 greased or paper-lined 2½-inch muffin cups. Bake at 350°F for 25 to 30 minutes, or until toothpick inserted in center comes out clean. Remove muffins from pan to wire rack. Serve warm or at room temperature. Makes 12 muffins.

Pumpkin Pancakes

Ingredients:
1 cup cooked pumpkin
2 eggs
1½ pints milk
Salt
Flour (enough to make a good batter)
2 teaspoons baking powder

Directions:
Mix together the cooked and cooled pumpkin, eggs, milk, baking powder, a little salt, and flour to make good batter. Beat until smooth and cook on the griddle.

Honey-Pumpkin Muffins with Cream Cheese Frosting

(Courtesy of the National Honey Board)

Ingredients:

2 cups all-purpose flour
1½ teaspoons ground
cinnamon
1 teaspoon baking soda
½ teaspoon salt
½ cup chopped walnuts
1 cup solid-pack pumpkin
1 cup honey
¼ cup vegetable oil

2 eggs, at room temperature,
slightly beaten
¼ cup low-fat buttermilk
1 teaspoon vanilla extract

Cream cheese frosting:

1 (8 oz.) package cream cheese
⅓ cup honey

Directions:

In a large bowl, stir together flour, cinnamon, baking soda and salt. Stir in walnuts. In a separate bowl, blend pumpkin, honey, oil, eggs, buttermilk and vanilla until smooth. Pour pumpkin mixture over dry ingredients. Stir just until mixed. Spoon batter into paper lined muffin cups, filling each to just below the rim. Bake at 350°F for about 25 minutes or until a toothpick inserted near the center of muffins comes out clean. Let pan cool on rack for 5 minutes. Remove muffins from pan and let cool on rack completely. Frost with Cream Cheese Frosting, if desired. Makes 12 muffins.

Frosting is optional on these muffins. Without it, they are ideal for breakfast; with it, they become a sweet afternoon snack.

Cream cheese frosting:

In a small bowl, with electric mixer, beat cream cheese (softened to room temperature) with honey, until fluffy.

Orange Wheat Muffins with Cream Cheese

Ingredients:

1 cup unbleached all-purpose flour
½ cup whole wheat flour
½ cup flaxseed meal
⅓ cup honey
1 teaspoon baking soda
1 tablespoon baking powder
¼ teaspoon salt
1 teaspoon orange extract
1 teaspoon orange zest
2 large eggs

2 tablespoons canola oil
½ cup pumpkin puree
1 cup plain low-fat yogurt
12 tablespoons low-fat cream cheese
12 teaspoons pumpkin seeds
Pumpkin pie spices or cinnamon to taste (optional)

You may substitute 2 eggs with 4 egg whites.

Careful, this recipe may have a laxative effect.

Muffin freezes very well when wrapped individually in plastic and placed in a freezer bag.

Directions:

Preheat the oven to 375°F. Blend the flours, flaxseed meal, honey, baking soda, baking powder, and salt in a mixing bowl. Blend in the orange extract, orange zest, canola oil, eggs, pumpkin puree, yogurt, and mix well. Fill muffin pan and bake for 25 minutes or until cooked through and golden brown.

Top each muffin with 1 tablespoon of low-fat cream cheese. Sprinkle spices or cinnamon, pumpkin seeds, and serve immediately.

Pumpkin Bread

(Contributed by Chef Nancy Berkoff, The Vegetarian Resource
Group, Vegetarian Journal, www.vrg.org)

Ingredients:

Vegetable oil spray
3 cups unbleached flour
½ teaspoon baking powder
1 teaspoon baking soda
1 teaspoon cinnamon
1 teaspoon nutmeg
1 teaspoon cloves
1 teaspoon ginger
2 cups sugar (use your
favorite vegan variety)

1 cup brown sugar (use your
favorite vegan variety)
¾ cup oil or mashed bananas
½ cup soft tofu
2 cups canned pumpkin (not
sweetened or spiced) or 2
cups stewed and pureed fresh
pumpkin
1 cup raisins
½ cup chopped walnuts
(optional)

Makes two 8-inch loaves or
twenty-four 2-tablespoon
muffins.

Pumpkin has lots of fiber and
nutrients and adds a pleasant
texture to many foods.

This pumpkin bread is just
sweet enough to serve toasted
for breakfast or for dessert, yet
it is savory enough to serve at
lunch or dinner.

Directions:

Preheat oven to 350°F.
Spray two small loaf pans
or place insert paper into
24 muffin cups.

Sift together flour, baking
powder, baking soda, and
spices. In a mixer bowl,
mix together sugars, oil
or bananas, and tofu. Add
pumpkin and mix well. Mixing on slow speed, gradually add
flour and mix until well combined. Add in raisins and nuts.

Pour into prepared pans. Bake for 45 minutes or until a knife
inserted in the center comes out clean. Allow to cool completely
before removing from pan. Makes two 8-inch loaves or twenty-
four 2-tablespoon muffins.

Pumpkin Waffles with Blueberries and Pomegranate Coulis

Ingredients:

2 cups flour, sifted

4 tablespoons turbinado sugar (or light brown sugar)

1 tablespoon baking powder

1 teaspoon baking soda

¼ teaspoon salt

1 tablespoon pumpkin pie spice

2 extra large eggs

1¾ cups buttermilk

½ cup pumpkin puree

2 tablespoons melted butter

1¼ cup blueberry juice (no sugar added)

1¼ cup pomegranate juice (no sugar added)

While making a large portion of waffles, you can keep them warm in a 270°F preheated oven.

Directions:

Place the juices and 1 tablespoon sugar in a pan. Bring to simmer over medium heat and reduce to 1 cup. Remove from heat and set aside to cool.

Mix the flour, 3 tablespoons sugar, baking powder, baking soda, salt, and spices together in a large bowl. In another bowl, whisk the egg yolks and buttermilk until frothy. Blend in the pumpkin puree and melted butter. Pour the mixture over the dry ingredients and mix until incorporated. Whisk the egg whites until set and gently fold into the prepared mixture.

Preheat a waffle iron, according to manufacturer's recommendations. Quickly spread batter to the rim and cook until the steaming stops and until the waffle is golden brown. Repeat with the remaining batter. Serve each waffle with 2 tablespoons of coulis.

Makes 8 waffles.

Homemade Granola
with Pumpkin Yogurt

Ingredients:

Yogurt
½ cup low-fat yogurt
1 tablespoon pumpkin puree

Granola
¼ cup honey
¼ cup vegetable oil
2 teaspoons pumpkin pie spice

1 teaspoon almond extract
½ teaspoon orange extract
3½ cups old fashioned oats, uncooked
¼ cup sliced almonds
¼ cup chopped walnuts

Directions:

Mix ½ cup low-fat yogurt and 1 tablespoon pumpkin puree for every ½ cup of granola.

Preheat the oven to 350°F. In a bowl, mix the honey, oil, spices, and extracts. Stir in the oats and nuts. Mix well and spread over a greased cookie sheet. Bake for 10 minutes. Stir and continue to bake for another 10 minutes or until golden brown. Cool completely and break apart.

Makes 10 (½ cup) servings.

Pumpkin Butter on Toast

Ingredients:

1 (15 oz.) can pumpkin puree
Zest (large strips) of one
orange
6 ounces freshly squeezed
orange juice
1 tablespoon frozen orange
concentrate
1 tablespoon pumpkin pie spices
Chopped pecans or walnuts,
slightly toasted for stronger flavor
Whole wheat bread slices, toasted

For a fun afternoon snack,
add some semi-sweet
chocolate chips to the recipe.

Directions:

Place the large strips of orange zest in a pan and cover with
water. Bring to boil over high heat. Reduce heat and simmer for
10 minutes. Drain and mince the zest.

Place the pumpkin puree, minced zest, orange juice, orange concentrate, and spices in a saucepan. Bring to boil over medium
heat. Reduce heat and simmer for 20 minutes, stirring occasionally with a wooden spoon to avoid burning on the bottom. Check
the flavor and adjust with more spices, if needed. Continue to
cook until thickened. Remove from heat and cool. Transfer to a
sanitized glass jar and refrigerate.

Top 1 slice of toasted bread with pumpkin butter and toasted
pecans or walnuts.

Makes approximately 2 cups of pumpkin butter.

Soups

Hearty Pumpkin Soup

Ingredients:

3 pounds pumpkin
1 teaspoon olive oil
2 large onions, sliced (about 1 pound)
1 garlic clove, minced
6 cups gluten-free chicken stock
2 cups low-fat milk
2 fresh sage leaves
1 teaspoon freshly minced thyme
3 tablespoons low-fat Greek yogurt
2 tablespoons pumpkin seeds
Salt and pepper to taste

Directions:

Peel the pumpkin and cut the flesh into medium cubes.

Heat the oil in a large pan over high heat. Add the onions and sauté until translucent. Add the pumpkin, garlic, stock, milk, sage, and thyme, and bring to a boil. Reduce heat, cover, and simmer for 30 minutes. Puree the vegetables in a blender using just enough cooking liquid to obtain a creamy consistency. Return to the pan and season with salt and pepper. Stir in the yogurt, garnish with the pumpkin seeds, and serve immediately.

Pumpkin Soup

(Contributed by Chef Nancy Berkoff, The Vegetarian Resource
Group, Vegetarian Journal, www.vrg.org)

The pumpkin gives this recipe a 'creamy' appearance and taste.

Ingredients:
3 cups canned pumpkin (not sweetened or spiced) or stewed
and pureed fresh pumpkin
2 cups vegetable stock
1 tablespoon non-hydrogenated vegan margarine
1 tablespoon flour
1 tablespoon vegan brown sugar
1 teaspoon black pepper
½ teaspoon lemon zest

Directions:
Combine pumpkin and stock together in a medium pot and allow mixture to simmer. Combine margarine and flour to make
a "roux" (thickening agent). Slowly beat the roux into the
pumpkin, stirring until smooth. Add sugar, pepper, and zest. Stir
and allow soup to simmer until heated. Makes twelve 4-ounce
servings.

Vegetable Soup

Ingredients:
2 quarts soup stock (8 or 10 cups)
3 cups mixed vegetables (pumpkin, string beans, celery, green peas, turnips, cauliflower, summer squash, onions, asparagus)
1 tomato
Parsnip, cabbage, potatoes (optional)
1 cup water
1 tablespoon corn starch
Seasonings

Directions:
To make the stock, use the liquid in which any type of meat has been boiled (corned beef, chicken, rabbit, mutton, or beef shank work best). Strain the liquid into a soup pot and boil over medium heat.

Cut vegetables into small cubes (turnips, carrots, pumpkin, celery, string beans, onion, summer squash, and cauliflower). Boil the hard vegetables, such as carrots, pumpkin, turnips, onions, string beans, and celery, before adding them to the pot. Strain and place them in the boiling stock. Add the softer vegetables like cauliflower, asparagus heads, and peas directly into the pot of stock. Lastly, add a diced red tomato. Dissolve one tablespoon of corn starch in a cup of water and pour it into the soup. Season to taste with salt and pepper and stir often. Allow the soup to cook until all ingredients are well-cooked.

African Pumpkin and Bean Soup

Ingredients:
1 can white beans
1 small onion, finely chopped
1 cup water
15 ounces fresh pumpkin puree
1½ cups apple juice
½ teaspoon cinnamon
⅛ teaspoon nutmeg, allspice, or ginger
½ teaspoon black pepper
¼ teaspoon salt
1 tablespoon chives

Directions:
Blend white beans, onion, and water with a potato masher or in a blender until smooth. In a large pot, add the pumpkin, juice, cinnamon, nutmeg, black pepper, and salt. Stir. Add the blended bean mixture to the pot. Cook over low heat for 15-20 minutes until warmed through.

Pumpkin Curry Soup

Ingredients:
1 tablespoon butter
1 cup finely chopped onion
2 garlic cloves, finely chopped
1 cup diced celery
1 teaspoon curry powder
⅛ teaspoon ground coriander
⅛ teaspoon crushed red pepper
3 cups water
1 cup low sodium chicken broth
32 ounces fresh pumpkin puree
1 cup fat-free half-and-half

Tip:

Soup may be prepared the day ahead. Cool to room temperature after adding pumpkin and half-and-half. Cover and refrigerate. Just before serving, blend then reheat to serving temperature, but do not boil.

Directions:

Melt butter in large saucepan over medium-high heat. Add onion, celery, and garlic; cook for 3 to 5 minutes or until tender. Stir in curry powder, coriander and crushed red pepper; cook for 1 minute. Add water and broth; bring to a boil. Reduce heat to low; cook, stirring occasionally, for 15 to 20 minutes to develop flavors. Stir in pumpkin and half-and-half; cook for 5 minutes or until heated through. Transfer mixture to food processor or blender (in batches, if necessary); cover. Blend until creamy. Serve warm or reheat to desired temperature. Garnish with dollop of sour cream and chives.

SOUPS

Pumpkin Pistachio Soup

Ingredients:
1 small, fresh red chili
3 tablespoons sugar
1¼ cups whole, shelled California pistachios
1½ pounds seeded fresh pumpkin
2 shallots
2 stalks lemon grass (available in large supermarkets or Asian specialty stores)
1 tablespoon butter or margarine
3 cups vegetable stock
¼ teaspoon ground white pepper
¼ teaspoon ground cloves
6 tablespoons light sour cream or crème fraîche
Fresh cilantro

Directions:
Seed and finely chop chili. Melt sugar in skillet until it is a light brown caramel color. Add chili and pistachios and stir to coat. Turn mixture out of pan onto foil or wax paper and let cool. Pare pumpkin and cut into cubes. Peel and chop shallots. Cut lemon grass into 4-inch lengths. Melt butter in large saucepan, add shallots and lemon grass, cover and cook 1 minute. Add cubed pumpkin, stock, pepper and cloves. Cover and simmer over low heat for 15 to 20 minutes or until tender. Discard lemon grass. Puree pumpkin mixture in food processor or electric blender. Return to saucepan. Whisk in sour cream, heat gently then pour into wide soup bowls. Top with cilantro and caramelized pistachios.

Vermicelli Soup

Ingredients:

6 quarts soup stock

5 cups minced vegetables (cabbage, pumpkin, onion, turnip, carrot, celery, squash—use part or all to suit taste)

6 ounces (2-3 cups) vermicelli, broken small

Directions:

Place vegetables in the stock. Boil and season. Add vermicelli and allow to simmer. Variations to this soup may be made by substituting rice, barley, or noodles for the vermicelli.

Salads

Chicken Salad with Fruit

Ingredients:

5 ounces fresh mixed greens
12 ounces cooked chicken breasts (without skin), diced
1 avocado, diced
1 large apple, diced (about 6 ounces)
1 orange, peeled and wedged (about 6 ounces)
2 kiwis, peeled and sliced (about 6 ounces)
4 teaspoons pumpkin seeds
2 tablespoons olive oil
2 tablespoons lemon juice
1 tablespoon fresh salad herbs
Large pinch each curry and ginger
4 ounces reduced-fat goat cheese, sliced
Salt and pepper to taste

Directions:

In a bowl mix the oil, lemon, and herbs. Blend in the curry, ginger, and season to taste.

In a bowl mix the greens with ⅔ of the prepared dressing. Equally divide the greens among four plates. Top with the chicken, fruit, avocado, pumpkin seeds, and goat cheese. Drizzle the remaining dressing and serve immediately.

Fruit and Pumpkin Salad

Ingredients:

1 small red onion, chopped
1 small cucumber, cut
lengthwise and sliced
2 oranges, peeled and
segmented
2 apples
1 lemon, juiced
¾ pound pumpkin meat,
medium diced
¼ teaspoon Dijon mustard

4 tablespoons olive oil
2 tablespoons cider vinegar
½ teaspoon garlic clove, minced
2 tablespoons freshly minced
basil
1 tablespoon freshly minced
mint
2 tablespoons chopped pecans
Salt and pepper to taste

Directions:

Peel, core, and slice the apples.
Transfer to a bowl, mix with the
lemon juice, and set aside.

You may serve this salad
with broiled or baked
salmon.

Mix the mustard, oil, cider
vinegar, garlic clove, basil, and
mint in a large serving bowl.

Season to taste before topping with the chopped red onion, sliced
cucumber, segmented oranges, and drained apples. Set aside
without mixing.

Place the pumpkin in a saucepan, cover with water, and add a
few pinches of salt. Bring to boil over high heat. Reduce heat
and continue to simmer until tender, about 10 to 15 minutes.
Strain and cool slightly before use. Mix the prepared salad with
the dressing and divide among four plates. Top with the warm
pumpkin, chopped pecans, and serve immediately.

Makes 4 servings.

Beets and Pumpkin Salad

Ingredients:

6 ounces baby spinach, washed and pat dry
1 small red onion, chopped
2 red beets
¾ pound pumpkin meat, diced
¼ teaspoon Dijon mustard
4 tablespoons olive oil
2 tablespoons cider vinegar
½ teaspoon garlic clove, minced
2 tablespoons freshly minced herbed salads
2 tablespoons pumpkin seeds
Olive oil
Salt and pepper to taste

Directions:

Preheat the oven to 375°F.

Mix the mustard, oil, cider vinegar, garlic, and herbs in a large serving bowl. Season to taste and top with the baby spinach. Add the chopped onion and set aside without mixing.

You may serve this salad with cooked turkey or chicken slices.

Place the diced pumpkin on a cookie sheet. Sprinkle olive oil and season to taste. Bake for 40 minutes or until tender.

Place the beets in a saucepan and cover with water. Bring to a boil over high heat. Reduce heat and simmer for 40 minutes or until tender. Strain and let cool a bit. Peel the beets, cut in half, and slice them.

Once the pumpkin is cooked, add the beets to the salad and mix with the dressing. Divide among four plates. Top each plate with the baked pumpkin, sprinkle the seeds, and serve immediately.

Makes 4 servings.

Curly Endive with Bacon and Pumpkin

Ingredients:

2 teaspoons grapeseed oil
8 ounces curly endive, washed and pat dry
12 cooked Brussels sprouts
6 ounces thick bacon slices, sliced into ¼-inch cut
¾ pound pumpkin meat, diced
1 small shallot, minced
2 tablespoons cider vinegar
4 tablespoons olive oil
2 tablespoons freshly minced salad herbs
Salt and pepper to taste

Directions:

In a bowl, mix the shallot, vinegar, olive oil, herbs, and season to taste.

Heat the grapeseed oil and quickly sauté the diced pumpkin in a pan over medium heat. Reduce heat and continue to cook for 10-15 minutes or until tender, mixing occasionally.

In another pan, sauté the bacon until barely golden brown. Add the cooked Brussels sprouts and continue to cook for 2 minutes. Mix a little bacon fat with the pumpkin at the end of the cooking time and also with the prepared dressing. Drain the bacon strips and Brussels sprouts from the remaining rendered fat.

Mix the curly endive with the dressing and equally divide among four plates. Top with the warm bacon, Brussels sprouts, diced pumpkin, and serve immediately.

Makes 4 servings.

Quinoa and Pumpkin Seeds Salad

Ingredients:

1 cup quinoa
2 teaspoons olive oil
1 small yellow onion, diced
1 large garlic clove, minced
2 large carrots, diced
¾ pound diced pumpkin meat
¼ cup freshly squeezed orange juice
¼ cup olive oil
2 tablespoons minced fresh ginger
1 teaspoon ground cumin
1 teaspoon ground cardamom
¼ cup sultana raisins
¼ cup toasted pumpkin seeds
Salt and cayenne pepper
Boston lettuce leaves (enough to cover serving platter)
Freshly minced parsley, for decoration

Directions:

In a bowl, mix the orange juice, ¼ cup of olive oil, 1 tablespoon ginger, ½ teaspoon ground cumin, ½ teaspoon ground cardamom, and season to taste. Set aside for later use.

Place a coffee filter into a fine mesh sieve. Rinse the quinoa under cold water through the filter.

Heat 2 teaspoons of olive oil in a saucepan over medium heat. Add the onion, garlic, carrots, pumpkin, and quickly sauté. Add 2 cups of water, quinoa, remaining ginger, remaining spices, and bring to a boil. Reduce heat and simmer for 20 minutes or until the liquid is completely evaporated.

Mix the cooked quinoa with the dressing and refrigerate for an hour.

Spread the quinoa over to the prepared serving platter. Top with the raisins and pumpkin seeds.

Sprinkle parsley and serve immediately.

Makes 4 servings.

Carrot, Apple, and Jícama Salad

Ingredients:

2 large carrots, peeled
1 small jícama, peeled
1 apple, peeled
4 tablespoons lemon juice
4 tablespoons light olive oil
2 tablespoons chopped cilantro
1 teaspoon sugar
¼ cup pumpkin seeds
Salt and pepper to taste

Directions:

In a bowl, mix the lemon juice, oil, cilantro, sugar, and season to taste.

Shred the carrots, jícama, and apple. Transfer to the dressing bowl and mix well. Top with the pumpkin seeds and serve immediately.

Makes 4 servings.

Chicken Caesar Salad

Ingredients:

8 ounces romaine lettuce
4 cooked skinless chicken
breast, sliced
8 tablespoons Caesar dressing
4 tablespoons freshly grated
Parmesan cheese
4 tablespoons pumpkin seeds

You may substitute shrimp
for the chicken.

Directions:

Preheat a broiler. Spread the pumpkin seeds on a cookie sheet.
Place under the broiler and slightly brown for a minute or so.

Mix the romaine with 6 tablespoons of the dressing. Equally
divide among four plates. Mix the chicken with the remaining
dressing. Top the prepared plates with the cooked chicken.

Sprinkle the Parmesan, toasted pumpkin seeds, and serve immediately.

Grilled Steak and Vegetable Salad

Ingredients:

2 large beef sirloin steaks
8 ounces mixed greens
1 red bell pepper, seeded and sliced
1 yellow bell pepper, seeded and sliced
1 small red onion, sliced
¼ cup cooked corn kernels
2 large tomatoes, sliced

¼ cup pumpkin seeds
1 jalapeño, seeded and chopped
1 handful cilantro, washed and pat dry
2 garlic cloves, minced
¼ cup olive oil
1 lime, juiced
Vegetable stock (or water)
Salt and pepper to taste

Directions:

Liquefy the pumpkin seeds, jalapeño, cilantro, garlic, oil, and lime juice in a blender. Add enough stock to reach a dressing consistency. Season to taste and set aside.

Divide the greens and vegetables among four plates. Refrigerate until use.

Preheat a grill. Lightly oil the rack of the grill. Brush oil over the steaks and season with pepper.

Add the steaks to the rack and close the grill. Cook for 4 minutes and turn over. Continue to cook, covered, for another 3 to 4 minutes for medium rare. Season with salt, transfer the steaks to a plate, and cover with aluminum foil. Wait 10 minutes before slicing.

Remove prepared plates from the refrigerator. Divide the sliced steaks among the four plates, drizzle the prepared dressing, and serve immediately.

Makes 4 servings.

Meat & Poultry Entrées

Grilled Steak with Pumpkin Puree

Ingredients:
4 beef sirloin steaks
4 medium potatoes, peeled and chopped
6 ounces pumpkin meat, chopped
1 tablespoon butter
¼ cup milk
Salt and pepper to taste

Directions:
Place potatoes in a pan and cover with water. Bring to a boil over high heat. Reduce heat and simmer for 5 minutes. Add the chopped pumpkin and continue to cook for 15 to 20 minutes or until very tender. Strain and transfer to a bowl. Add the butter and milk. Mash with a potato masher and season to taste.

Meanwhile preheat a grill. Lightly oil the rack of the grill. Brush oil over the steaks and season with pepper. Add the steaks to the rack and close the grill. Cook for 4 minutes then turn over.

Cover and continue to cook for another 3 to 4 minutes for medium rare. Season with salt and serve immediately with the pumpkin puree.

Makes 4 servings.

Harvest Beef Stew

Ingredients:

2 tablespoons grapeseed oil
2 pounds beef stew meat, cubed
1 large onion, diced
2 carrots, diced
2 garlic cloves, minced
1 celery stalk, diced
1½ cups beef stock
½ cup pumpkin puree
1½ cups medium diced pumpkin meat

½ cup corn kernels
¼ cup dry apricots
¼ cup prunes
Salt and pepper to taste

Directions:

Soak the apricots and prunes in warm water for an hour.

Place the beef cubes in a plastic bag with the flour. Add a couple pinches of salt and pepper. Shake well and transfer half to a casserole dish that has been heated with 1 tablespoon of oil over medium high heat. Brown the beef cubes on all sides. Remove from pan and set aside.

Repeat with the remaining oil and beef cubes. Add the beef that was set aside, along with the onion, carrots, garlic, and celery. Briefly sauté. Add the stock, pumpkin puree, and bring to a boil. Reduce heat, cover, and continue to simmer for 65 minutes. Add the pumpkin meat, corn, drained apricot, drained prunes, and continue to simmer uncovered for 25 minutes. Adjust seasonings and serve immediately.

Makes 4 to 6 servings.

Fall Caramelized Pork Tenderloin

Ingredients:

1 tablespoon butter
1¼ pound pork tenderloin
1 (32 oz.) bottle apple juice
2 to 3 tablespoons maple syrup
1 teaspoon cinnamon
¾ pound pumpkin meat, chopped
1 large apple, chopped
2 tablespoons crème fraîche
Salt and pepper to taste

Directions:

Sprinkle the pork tenderloin with cinnamon and place in a dish. Cover with apple juice and refrigerate for an hour.

Heat the butter in a saucepan over medium heat. Add the pumpkin meat and apple, and sauté quickly. Add ¼ cup apple juice, 1 teaspoon cinnamon, and bring to a boil. Reduce heat and simmer for 15 minutes. Cook until the liquid is evaporated and the pumpkin cooked through. Transfer to a bowl and mash with a fork. Add the crème fraîche and season to taste.

Meanwhile preheat the oven broiler. Drain tenderloin and place it in a greased ovenproof dish. Brush it with maple syrup and sprinkle cinnamon. Place the dish on a rack 4 inches away from the broiler. Broil for 6 minutes, turn over, and continue to broil for another 5 minutes. Remove from the oven and let rest 5 minutes covered with aluminum foil. Slice and serve with the creamed pumpkin.

Makes 4 servings.

Lamb Tagine

Ingredients:

2 tablespoons grapeseed oil
2 tablespoons clarified butter
2 pounds deboned lamb
shoulder, cubed
1 pumpkin (about 2 pounds),
seeded and chopped
2 onions, chopped
2 turnips, chopped
2 carrots, chopped
2 yellow zucchini, chopped
1 teaspoon ground cumin

1 teaspoon ground coriander
1 teaspoon ground ginger
1 teaspoon paprika
½ teaspoon cinnamon
Few saffron shreds
Bunch fresh coriander,
shredded
2 tablespoons honey
1 (6-7 oz.) package couscous
Salt and pepper to taste

Directions:

Heat one cup of water with the saffron shreds.

In a bowl mix the cumin, coriander, ginger, paprika, and cinnamon. Place the lamb meat in a plastic bag and mix with the prepared spices. Heat 1 tablespoon of oil in a Dutch oven over medium heat. Brown half the meat on all sides. Remove from pan and set aside. Repeat with the remaining oil and lamb cubes. Add the meat set aside, onions, turnips, carrots, and saffron water.

Cover and cook for an hour over low heat.

Heat the clarified butter in a pan over medium heat. Add the chopped pumpkin and brown on all sides. Add the honey and mix quickly. Transfer to the cooking meat, add the yellow zucchinis, and continue to cook for another half hour. Meanwhile cook the couscous according to package instructions.

Finish the tagine by adding the shredded fresh coriander, adjust seasonings, and serve immediately with the couscous.

Makes 4 servings.

Roasted Chicken
with Pumpkin Risotto

Ingredients:

1-4 pounds roasting chicken
2 tablespoons olive oil
12 ounces Arborio rice
4 to 5 cups chicken stock (low-fat and low-sodium)
4 ounces onions, diced (about 1 small onion, diced)
1 tablespoon garlic cloves, minced
8 ounces cooked diced pumpkin meat, hot
¼ cup Parmesan cheese, grated
¼ cup Chardonnay wine
¼ cup cream, hot
2 teaspoons dried thyme, minced
3 tablespoons fresh salad

Directions:

Preheat the oven to 325°F.

Remove giblets from the chicken. Rinse the chicken and pat dry. Season the chicken cavity with salt and pepper. Brush 1 tablespoon of olive oil all over the chicken and sprinkle 1 teaspoon of thyme over it. Place the chicken in a roasting pan and roast for 2 to 2½ hours or until the juices run clear.

Heat the remaining oil in a pan over high heat. Add the onions and sauté until translucent. Add the garlic, rice, and stir for 1 minute. Add the wine, remaining thyme, and cook until the liquid is evaporated over medium heat. Add half of the stock and simmer uncovered. Once the liquid is absorbed, add the remaining stock, and continue to simmer uncovered. Once the stock is almost absorbed, check the rice. It should be cooked through before going on. If not quite done, keep adding more stock and cook until almost evaporated again. Add the Parmesan, cream, herbs, season to taste, and bring to a simmer. Remove from heat, gently add the cooked diced pumpkin, and cover for 2 minutes before serving with the roasted chicken.

Makes 4 servings.

White Bean Ragoût with Chicken Sausage

Ingredients:

2 teaspoons olive oil
½ pound chicken sausage, largely sliced
1 cup dried white beans
2 slices bacon, sliced small
1 large onion, diced
2 large garlic cloves, minced
1½ cups canned tomatoes
½ cup pumpkin pureé
½ teaspoon dried Italian herbs
Salt and pepper to taste

Directions:

In a pan, cover the beans with water and bring to boil over high heat. Strain and set aside the beans for later use.

Heat half of the oil in a large saucepan and quickly sauté the bacon over medium heat. Add the onion and sauté for another minute. Add the garlic, beans, herbs, and enough water to largely cover the beans. Bring to a boil over medium high heat. Reduce heat and simmer for 30 minutes.

Add the tomatoes, pumpkin puree, and mix well. Bring to a boil and continue to simmer for another 10 minutes.

Meanwhile heat the remaining oil over high heat. Add the sausage pieces and brown on both sides. Once the bean ragout has cooked, add the sausage to it and continue to cook for another 10 minutes or until the beans are cooked through. Adjust seasonings and serve immediately.

Makes 4 servings.

Turkey Scaloppini Parmesan

Ingredients:

8 small turkey scaloppini
½ cup flour
4 eggs, beaten
1½ cups dried Italian
bread crumbs
4 tablespoons olive oil
2½ cups marina sauce
½ cup pumpkin puree
1 cup Parmigiano-Reggiano
cheese, grated

1 tablespoon freshly minced basil
1 tablespoon freshly minced
parsley
Salt and pepper to taste

This recipe can be served
with spaghetti.

Directions:

Preheat the oven broiler and place rack ten inches away from
the heating element.

Lightly season the scaloppini with pepper and salt.

Place the flour, eggs, and bread crumbs each into a shallow dish.
Dredge each scaloppini in flour, eggs, and finally bread crumbs.
Transfer to a cookie sheet covered with parchment paper.

Heat the pumpkin puree and thin out with a little water to obtain the same consistency as the marina sauce. Add the marina
sauce, herbs, and bring to a simmer. Adjust seasonings.

Heat half of the olive oil in a large skillet over high heat. Add 4
scaloppini and sauté until golden brown on both sides, turning
only once. Transfer to a large greased ovenproof pan and cover
with aluminum foil to keep warm. Repeat with the remaining
oil and scaloppini. Top the scaloppini with the prepared sauce
and then cheese. Place in the oven and broil until the cheese is
golden brown. Serve immediately.

Makes 4 servings.

Nutty Chicken Breast with Spinach

Ingredients:

3 tablespoons grapeseed oil
4 skinless chicken breasts
2 extra large egg whites
1 teaspoon salt
½ cup chopped almonds
⅓ cup pumpkin seeds
½ cup chopped walnuts
1 small yellow onion, sliced
1 garlic clove, minced

1 tablespoon freshly minced
ginger root
20 ounces fresh spinach,
trimmed
Salt and pepper to taste

Directions:

Place the almonds in a blender and chop. Repeat with the pumpkin seeds and the walnuts. Do not overdo it, as you do not want to end up with a flour consistency. Transfer the nuts and seeds to a flat dish. Place the egg whites in a flat dish and loosen them up with a fork.

Place each chicken breast between plastic wrap and slightly flatten with a meat pounder. Lightly season each chicken piece with salt and pepper. Dip each chicken piece into the egg whites and then into the nuts. Apply hand pressure to help it stick to the chicken. Transfer to a cookie sheet covered with parchment paper.

Heat 2 tablespoons of oil in a large pan over medium heat. Add the crusted chicken pieces and brown. Turn over and continue to cook over low-medium heat until cooked through, about 10 minutes from the beginning.

Meanwhile heat the remaining oil in a pan over medium high heat. Add the onion and sauté until translucent. Add the garlic, ginger, and spinach. Mix often and cook until the spinach is wilted. Serve immediately with the crusted chicken.

Makes 4 servings.

Pumpkin Sauce for Poultry

Ingredients:
1 pumpkin
2 tablespoons butter
½ teaspoon ginger
Juice 1 lemon or 1 tablespoon of cider vinegar
Sugar (optional)
Water

Directions:
Pare a pumpkin, cut in slices, and cut the slices in cubes. Add a little hot water, and let simmer on the back of the range all day. Then pass through a colander. To a pint of pulp add 2 tablespoons of butter, ½ teaspoon of ginger, the juice of a small lemon, or 2 tablespoons of cider vinegar, and a little sugar (optional). Let boil, and serve, hot or cold, with roast poultry.

Cilantro Pesto with Pumpkin Seeds

(Recipe courtesy of the World's Healthiest Food website,
www.WHFoods.org)

If you want to enhance the flavor of chicken or fish as well
as add extra vitamins K, A and C to your meal, try this pesto
that can be prepared in a matter of minutes. It's also a great
addition to fish tacos; top tacos with pesto and avocado for a
tasty treat. Enjoy!

Ingredients:

2 cups chopped fresh cilantro
1 cup chopped fresh parsley
3 scallions, chopped
4 cloves garlic, coarsely chopped
1 teaspoon ground cumin
2 or 3 canned jalapeños, depending on desired heat
½ cup coarsely chopped pumpkin seeds
2 tablespoons water
1 tablespoon fresh lemon juice
2 tablespoons extra virgin olive oil
Salt and white pepper to taste

Directions:

Chop garlic and let sit for 5 minutes to enhance its health-pro-
moting properties while you prepare the rest of the ingredients.

Blend all ingredients in a food processor or blender. Add olive
oil a little at a time at end. You want the pesto to be blended yet
not smooth. It is best with a little texture. Serve at room temperature. Do not heat it.

Seared Scallops with Pumpkin Timbale

Ingredients:

2 teaspoons olive oil
2 teaspoons butter
1 pound dry sea scallops
Salt and pepper to taste
Pumpkin timbale (see page 57)

Directions:

Rinse and pat dry the scallops. Lightly season the scallops with salt and pepper.

Heat the oil and butter in a large saucepan over medium-high heat. Add the scallops and cook until golden brown on both sides, about 2 minutes per side. Serve immediately with the timbale.

Makes 4 servings.

Grilled Halibut with Avocado Puree

Ingredients:
1 tablespoon olive oil
4 halibut fillets
2 ripe avocadoes
1 teaspoon Dijon mustard
½ teaspoon ground cumin
½ lime, juiced
4 tablespoons freshly minced cilantro
4 to 6 drops Tabasco
4 tablespoons pumpkin seeds
Salt and pepper to taste

Directions:
Preheat grill on medium high.

Mash the avocadoes with a fork. Mix in the cumin, lime juice, mustard, 2 tablespoons cilantro, Tabasco, and season to taste.

Brush oil over halibut fillets and lightly season with salt and pepper. Grease the rack of the grill. Add the fillets and grill for 3 to 5 minutes on each side. The fish will start to flake when it is done. Transfer the fillets to four plates and top with a dollop of avocado puree. Sprinkle remaining cilantro, spread pumpkin seeds, and serve immediately.

Makes 4 servings.

Mediterranean Seafood Stew

Ingredients:

1 tablespoon olive oil
1 small onion, julienned
1 green bell pepper, julienned
1 small fennel bulb, julienned
4 garlic cloves, minced
4 plum tomatoes, peeled,
seeded, and diced
¼ cup pumpkin puree
1 cup vegetable stock
⅓ cup dry white wine
½ of an orange, juiced
1 bouquet garni

Few saffron shreds
4 fish fillets
8 clams and 8 mussels,
scrubbed clean
8 shrimp, peeled and deveined
1 bunch of basil, minced
4 small pumpkin, emptied
Salt and pepper to taste

Directions:

Heat the oil in a deep saucepan over high heat. Add the onion and sauté until translucent. Add the pepper, fennel, garlic, and cook for five minutes. Mix in the tomatoes, pumpkin puree, stock, wine, orange juice, bouquet garni, saffron, and bring to a boil. Reduce heat and simmer for 5 minutes to concentrate the flavors. Add the fish and cook for another five minutes. Add the clams, mussels, shrimp, and cook until the shells open. Remove bouquet garni, add basil, and season to taste.

Place one small pumpkin per plate. Fill each pumpkin with the stew and serve immediately.

Makes 4 servings.

Shrimp with Pumpkin and Zucchini Fettuccini

Ingredients:

1 tablespoon olive oil
1 pound shrimp, peeled and deveined
6 ounces whole wheat fettuccini
2 strips bacon, sliced
1 medium onion, diced small
1 small leek, white part only, diced small
6 ounces pumpkin meat, diced small

6 ounces green zucchini, diced small
2 garlic cloves, minced
¼ cup white wine
4 ounces cream
2 tablespoons freshly minced basil
Salt and pepper to taste

Directions:

Cook the fettuccini according to package instructions.

Place the wine in a saucepan and reduce by half.

Heat the oil in a saucepan over high heat. Add the bacon and brown. Add the onion, leek, and sauté for a minute. Add the pumpkin, zucchini, garlic, shrimp, and lightly brown. Add reduced wine, cream, basil, and reduce to a creamy consistency. Strain the pasta and mix them with the mixture. Season to taste and serve immediately.

Makes 4 servings.

15-Minute Salmon with Tomato Salsa

(Recipe courtesy of the World's Healthiest Food website, www.WHFoods.org)

If you want a great tasting recipe that also provides over 100% of the daily value for hard-to-find omega-3 fatty acids and vitamin D, try this easy-to-prepare recipe tonight. It only takes 15 minutes and you will have a meal you'll want to share with your best friends. Enjoy!

Ingredients:

1½ pounds salmon fillet cut into 4 pieces, skin and bones removed
1 tablespoon lemon juice
Salt and pepper to taste

Salsa:

1 large fresh ripe tomato, seeds and excess pulp removed, diced small pieces, about ¼ inch
3 tablespoons finely minced onion

3 medium cloves garlic, pressed
1-2 tablespoons minced jalapeño pepper (or to taste)
1 tablespoon minced fresh ginger
1 tablespoon coarsely chopped pumpkin seeds
¼ cup chopped fresh cilantro
2 tablespoons lemon juice
1 tablespoon extra virgin olive oil
Salt and black pepper to taste

Healthy Cooking Tips:

The ingredients of the salsa blend together better if you chop them fine. Also, it is best to add just a little jalapeño at a time, so you can get it to your personal preference of chili heat, without making it too hot.

Directions:

To quick-broil preheat broiler on high and place an all stainless steel skillet (be sure the handle is also stainless steel) or cast iron pan under the heat for about 10 minutes to get it very hot. The pan should be 5 to 7 inches from the heat source.

Rub salmon with 1 tablespoon fresh lemon juice and a little salt and pepper. (You can quick-broil with the skin on; it just takes a minute or two longer. The skin will peel right off after cooking.)

Using a hot pad, pull pan away from heat and place salmon on hot pan, skin side down. Return to broiler. Keep in mind that it is cooking rapidly on both sides so it will be done very quickly, usually in 7 minutes depending on thickness (10 minutes for every inch of thickness). Test with a fork for doneness. It will flake easily when it is cooked. Salmon is best when it is still pink inside.

Salsa:

Combine all salsa ingredients. Spoon over salmon. Garnish with mint and a sprinkle of extra virgin olive oil. Serves 4.

Vegetarian Entrées

Pumpkin à la Parmesan

Ingredients:

1 large pumpkin
Butter
Grated nutmeg
Parmesan cheese
Salt to taste

Directions:

Cut a large pumpkin into square pieces and boil them for about
a quarter of an hour in salt and water. Drain them, and put
them in a pan with a little butter, salt, and grated nutmeg. Fry
them, and sprinkle with a little Parmesan cheese. Bake for a
short time in the oven until the cheese begins to melt, and then
serve while hot.

Squash with Pecans and Cranberries

Ingredients:

¼ cup pecans
1 tablespoon dried cranberries
½ cup boiling water
1 cup vegetable broth
1 cup diced or julienned butternut squash
1 cup diced or julienned acorn squash
1 cup diced or julienned pumpkin
2 tablespoons butter
Juice of 1 lemon
Salt and pepper as needed

Removing the rind from a hard-skin squash can be a challenge. Give yourself plenty of room to work, and be sure to cut a thin slice from the bottom or side of the squash to help it stay flat on the cutting board.

Directions:

Preheat the oven to 300°F. Place the pecans on a shallow baking pan and toast the pecans approximately 10 minutes, stirring occasionally, until brown. Set aside.

Combine the dried cranberries with boiling water. Allow them to plump for 10 to 15 minutes. Chop them coarsely and set aside.

Bring the broth to a boil over high heat in a skillet. Add the squash and pumpkin. Cover the skillet and simmer over low heat until tender, about 10 to 12 minutes. Remove the cover, increase the heat to high, and allow any excess moisture to cook away, about 2 to 3 minutes.

Drain the cranberries and add them to the skillet along with the pecans, butter, lemon juice, salt, and pepper. Continue to cook for another 2 minutes, stirring gently to distribute all of the ingredients evenly. Serve immediately.

Italian Fried Pumpkin

Ingredients:
Pumpkin
Flour
Egg
Olive oil
Salt and pepper to taste

Directions:
Take a slice of pumpkin, remove the rind and the seeds. Cut it into fine strips. Roll in flour and dip in egg, and fry in olive-oil. Season with salt and pepper.

Scalloped Pumpkin

Ingredients:
1 cup cooked pumpkin
½ teaspoon salt
⅛ teaspoon pepper
⅛ teaspoon ginger
2 tablespoons melted shortening
1 cup fine bread crumbs
2 eggs, well beaten

Directions:
Mix the pumpkin, seasonings, shortening and half the crumbs.
Add eggs and spread in shallow greased baking dish. Sprinkle
rest of crumbs over top. Bake 40 minutes in moderate oven
(400°F).

Vegetables alla Napoletana

Ingredients:

¼ onion
2 or 3 green peppers
1 eggplant
1 or 2 potatoes
Tomatoes
Pumpkin
Few tablespoons oil
Salt and pepper to taste

Directions:

Chop the onion and fry in oil. The other vegetables should be
in proportion to each other. For example, if there is a cupful of
each of the other vegetables when they are cut up, use a cupful
of tomatoes unless you wish the tomato flavor to be very pro-
nounced. Peel and cube the potatoes, eggplant and pumpkin. Remove the seeds and stems from the peppers and slice or shred
them coarsely. Add the tomatoes to the onion and oil. After that
has cooked a few minutes add the potatoes. When they are half
done, put in the peppers, lastly the eggplant, pumpkin, and salt
and pepper. Continue cooking until the vegetables are tender but
still whole and firm.

Mashed Pumpkin

Ingredients:
Pumpkin (1 pound feeds 6 people)
Butter
1 small onion
2 egg yolks (or 1 egg yolk and a spoonful of cream)

Directions:
Remove the seeds and the peel; cut in pieces; put into a sauce-pan with a cupful of water; cook an hour and a half over medium heat. Pass it through the strainer. In a sauce-pan, slightly brown a piece of butter as large as an egg; in it, brown a small onion chopped fine. Add the mashed pumpkin, and season with salt and pepper. Simmer for about 15 minutes. Thicken with two egg yolks, or one yolk and a spoonful of cream. Served with bread.

Vegetable Curry

Ingredients:

1 small onion
1 large potato
½ pint green peas
Butter or olive oil
1 tablespoon wheat flour
Water
1 teaspoon curry powder
1 teaspoon salt
Vegetables cut into small pieces (eggplant, tomatoes, okra, cucumbers, pumpkin or squash—use some or all of them)
Macaroni or bread bits (optional)

Directions:

Cut a small onion, or half a large one, into thin slices and put them with a piece of butter the size of an egg (or 4 tablespoons of olive oil), into a sauce-pan, and let them brown slightly. Pare a large potato, and cut it into thin slices, and wash them. When the onion is browned, add to it the potato and other vegetables, and cover the pan. Mix the wheat flour with a little water, so as not to become lumpy; then, add enough water to make about a cupful in all; and put in a teaspoon of curry-powder (more or less, according to taste) and a teaspoon of salt. Add this mixture to the vegetables, when they have cooked some fifteen minutes, and are almost soft; and, stirring all the time, or still better in a double boiler, let the whole cook gently an hour or so longer. Macaroni or bread bits may be added.

Mix the curry with boiled rice. The rice should be boiled in such a way as to be loose, though thoroughly cooked and soft. Instead of rice, hominy can also be used.

Pumpkin Baked Au Gratin

Ingredients:
Pumpkin, sliced
Tomato sauce
Grated cheese
Breadcrumbs
Butter

Directions:
Cut up a young pumpkin into rounds about ½-inch thick. Place these in a buttered pie-dish, cover with tomato sauce, sprinkle grated cheese over pretty thickly, then scatter breadcrumbs, with small bits of butter, on top. Bake in a moderate oven until the pumpkin is tender.

Stewed Pumpkin with Tomatoes

Ingredients:

3½ pounds pumpkin
1 medium-sized onion
1 quart stewed tomatoes, strained
1 tablespoon margarine
1 tablespoon cooking oil
1 tablespoon flour
¼ teaspoon pepper
2 teaspoons salt
Toast

Directions:

Wash and pare the pumpkin and cut into pieces about two inches square. Parboil it for ten minutes. Chop the onion and fry it until brown in the oil, using a stew-pan. Add the pumpkin, salt, and pepper, and cook for five minutes. Then cover the pumpkin with the tomato, and stew gently until the pumpkin is quite tender. Arrange the pumpkin on a hot dish and thicken the tomato with the margarine and the flour cooked together. Add more seasoning if needed and pour the sauce over the pumpkin. Garnish with thin, narrow strips of toast.

Pumpkin Timbale

Ingredients:

1 pound pumpkin meat, diced small
1 tablespoon grapeseed oil
4 to 5 ounces ricotta cheese
1 teaspoon vanilla extract
Large pinch ground cardamom
Large pinch ground nutmeg
2 eggs
Salt and pepper to taste

Directions:

Heat the oil and diced pumpkin in a pan over medium heat. Quickly sauté, cover, and reduce heat. Continue to cook for 10 minutes. Uncover and continue to cook over medium heat until the water is evaporated and the pumpkin very soft.

Preheat the oven to 375°F. Prepare a warm "bain-marie" (water bath) for the oven.

Transfer the pumpkin to a bowl and roughly mash. Add the ricotta cheese, vanilla extract, cardamom, nutmeg, eggs, a large pinch of salt, and pinch of pepper. Mash until well incorporated and then divide among four buttered ramekins. Place the ramekins in the warm bain-marie, making sure the water reaches only half of the height of the ramekins, and bake for 20 minutes.

Makes 4 servings.

Cabbage and Pumpkin Stir-Fry

Ingredients:

2 teaspoons grapeseed oil
1 large onion, diced
4 cups shredded purple cabbage
2 cups medium diced pumpkin meat
1 garlic clove, minced
1 tablespoon minced ginger root
2 green onions, chopped
2 tablespoons low sodium soy sauce

1 tablespoon rice vinegar
1 teaspoon sesame oil
1 tablespoon sesame seeds
Cornstarch mixed with a little water
Pepper to taste

Directions:

In a wok, heat the grapeseed oil over medium high heat. Add the onion and cook until translucent. Add garlic, ginger, pumpkin, and stir-fry for 8 minutes. Add the green onion, cabbage and a little water to avoid burning. Cook for 5 minutes or until the pumpkin is soft. Add soy sauce and gently mix. Thicken with cornstarch and water mixture. Drizzle with sesame oil, season with pepper, and serve immediately.

Makes 4 servings.

Stuffed Poblano Chilies

Ingredients:

2 teaspoons olive oil
4 poblano chilies
1 medium onion, diced
2 tomatoes, seeded and diced
1 cup cooked black beans
1 cup cooked corn kernels
2 garlic cloves, minced
1 jalapeño, seeded and diced
½ cup toasted pumpkin seeds
½ cup chopped cilantro
1 teaspoon ground cumin
1¼ cup Monterey Jack cheese, shredded
Salt and pepper to taste

You may also cook the stuffed chilies in the oven at 375°F for 15 to 20 minutes.

Directions:

Preheat the grill on medium.

Cut and slice the chilies in half. Scrape out the seeds and set aside.

Heat the oil in a saucepan over high heat. Add the onion and sauté until translucent. Add garlic and sauté 1 minute. Add the tomatoes, black beans, corn, jalapeño, pumpkin seeds, cilantro, cumin, and cook until hot. Divide mixture among the chile halves and top with the cheese.

Lightly oil the rack of the grill and place the stuffed chilies on the grill. Grill for 15 to 20 minutes or until the cheese is golden brown and the chilies cook through. If they start to burn, move them away from the heat source to finish cooking and then serve immediately.

Makes 4 servings.

Pumpkin in Ginger Coconut Sauce

Ingredients:

1 pound pumpkin meat, medium diced
1 tablespoon grapeseed oil
8 scallions, sliced
1 inch fresh ginger root, minced
1 jalapeño pepper, seeded and minced
1 (15 oz.) can unsweetened coconut milk

1 teaspoon red curry paste
2 tablespoons freshly minced cilantro
Salt and pepper to taste

Try serving this dish over rice.

Directions:

Heat the oil in a saucepan over medium high heat. Add the pumpkin meat and sauté until slightly brown. Add the scallions, ginger, jalapeño, coconut milk, curry paste, cilantro, and bring to a boil. Reduce heat and continue to cook until the pumpkin is tender, about 15 minutes. Add a little water, if the milk thickens too much. Adjust seasoning and serve immediately.

Makes 4 servings.

Fried Potato and Pumpkin Cakes

Ingredients:

1 ½ cups cooked mashed potatoes
½ cup pumpkin puree
1 egg, beaten
¼ cup flour, sifted
1 tablespoon freshly minced parsley
Salt and pepper to taste

Directions:

Mix the mashed potatoes and pumpkin puree in a bowl (mixture should be on the dry side). If mixture is too moist, place in a nonstick pan over low heat and dry the mixture slowly, mixing constantly to avoid burning. Remove from heat and completely cool. Add the egg, flour, parsley, and season to taste. Mix well and then form patties. Fry in a little oil until golden brown on both sides and serve immediately.

Makes 4 servings.

Thanksgiving Pumpkin Crumble

Ingredients:

2½ cups pumpkin meat, diced
3 slices bacon, thinly sliced
1 tablespoon pumpkin pie spice
6 ounces shredded cheddar cheese
2 tablespoons crème fraîche
2 tablespoons freshly minced parsley
6 tablespoons flour
2 ounces chestnut flour
3 ounces butter, diced and cold
½ cup roasted chopped pecans
Salt and pepper to taste

Directions:

Preheat the oven to 400°F.

Sauté the bacon until golden brown in a pan over medium high heat. Strain and set aside to cool.

Preheat a steamer and add the pumpkin. Cook for 15 minutes or until barely tender. Transfer to a bowl. Mix in the cooked bacon, spices, 3 ounces of cheddar, crème fraîche, pecans, and season to taste. Transfer to a buttered ovenproof dish. In a bowl, crumble by hand the flours, butter, and remaining cheddar. Crumble over the puree, sprinkle parsley, and bake for 20 to 30 minutes or until the crust is cooked and golden brown.

Makes 4 servings.

Side Dishes
& Snacks

Cooked Pumpkin

Ingredients:

1 medium pumpkin

Directions:

Preheat oven to 300°F. Cut pumpkin into small manageable pieces and cut off pith and seeds. Place cut pumpkin, skin side up,
in a large roasting pan. Add ¼ cup water, and bake uncovered
for 1 hour or until tender. Remove from oven, and allow pumpkin to cool. When cooled, cut away skin, and mash or puree the
pumpkin flesh. Use in any recipe that calls for canned pureed
pumpkin.

Roasted Pumpkin Seeds

Roasted pumpkin seeds make an excellent healthy snack, salad topping, or nutty addition to many fish dishes.

Ingredients:
Pumpkin seeds
Olive oil (or melted butter)
Salt to taste (optional)

Pumpkin seeds may be roasted in the hull or can be removed first.

Directions:
Remove the seeds from the pumpkin and place them in a bowl of warm water. Clean them gently to remove any excess flesh or strings. Drain the seeds in a colander, and lay them to dry on a towel. Once they are dry, heat the oven to 275-300°F. Place the seeds in a single layer on a baking pan, drizzle them with olive oil (or melted butter), and season them with salt (optional). Roast the pumpkin seeds for about 1 hour, stirring frequently. Allow them to cool. Store them in the refrigerator in an airtight container to maintain freshness.

Pumpkin Hummus

(Courtesy of the National Honey Board)

Ingredients:

1 tablespoon tahini
2 teaspoons extra virgin olive oil
2 tablespoons lemon juice
2-3 tablespoons water
1 teaspoon ground cumin
½ teaspoon sea salt, or to taste
1 (15 oz.) can garbanzo beans, drained
15 ounces fresh pumpkin puree
1 clove garlic, minced

Directions:

In a blender, combine all ingredients and puree until smooth.
Add a bit of extra water if the mixture is too thick to blend.
Makes about 2 cups. Serve on toasted whole wheat pita triangles
or with fresh vegetables.

Broccoli with Pumpkin Hummus

Ingredients:

2 teaspoons flaxseed oil
1 tablespoon lemon juice
1 teaspoon ground cumin
½ teaspoon ground coriander
2 cups cooked garbanzo beans
2 cups cooked pumpkin purée
1 garlic clove, pureed
1 teaspoon paprika
3 pounds broccoli
Salt to taste

Directions:

Combine all the ingredients, except the broccoli florets, in a food processor.

Mix until very smooth and thin out with water as needed. Serve with broccoli florets.

Honey Pumpkin Tea Bread
(Courtesy of the National Honey Board

Ingredients:

½ cup (1 stick) unsalted butter, at room temperature, plus additional for the pan
2 cups all-purpose flour
1 teaspoon baking soda
½ teaspoon salt
½ teaspoon ground cinnamon
½ teaspoon ginger
½ teaspoon grated nutmeg
1 cup honey
1 cup fresh pumpkin puree
2 eggs, room temperature
2 teaspoons lemon juice
1 teaspoon vanilla extract

Directions:

Preheat oven to 350°F. Position rack in center of oven. Generously butter a 9-inch x 5-inch metal loaf pan and set aside.
Sift flour, baking soda, salt, cinnamon, ginger and nutmeg into a medium bowl. Set aside. In a large bowl, combine butter and honey and beat with an electric mixer at medium speed for 2 minutes or until smooth. Add the pumpkin; beat for 1 minute or until well combined. Beat in eggs one at a time, beating each for 1 minute. Stir in lemon juice and vanilla extract. Add the sifted dry ingredients. With the mixer on low, beat just until incorporated. Increase mixer speed to medium and beat for 2 minutes or until the batter is smooth, scraping down the sides of the bowl as necessary with a rubber spatula. Spread into prepared pan. Bake about 65 minutes, or until a cake tester or wooden skewer inserted into the middle of the loaf comes out clean. Cool the bread on a wire rack for 10 minutes, slide out of mold, and continue cooling on the rack for 30 minutes before cutting. Makes 1 loaf.

Sweet Pumpkin Pickles

Ingredients:
Pumpkin
2 quarts vinegar
4 cups sugar
2 tablespoon mixed spices (whole cloves, cinnamon, whole allspice, ginger)

Directions:
Peel the pumpkin and remove the seeds, cut in strips ½-inch thick and about three inches long. Make a syrup of two quarts of vinegar, four cups of sugar, more if wanted sweeter, two tablespoonfuls mixed spices and boil until clear, but not until they fall to pieces. Place pumpkin slices upright in sterilized glass jars and pour the syrup over them. Seal the jars.

Pumpkin Indian Cakes

Ingredients:
Stewed pumpkin
Corn meal
Butter

Directions:
Take equal portions of corn meal, and stewed pumpkin that has been well mashed and drained very dry in a sieve or colander. Put the stewed pumpkin into a pan, and stir the meal gradually into it, a spoonful at a time, adding a little butter as you proceed. Mix the whole thoroughly, stirring it very hard. If not thick enough to form a stiff dough, add a little more corn meal. Make it into round, flat cakes, about the size of a muffin, and bake them on a hot griddle greased with butter. Or lay them in a square iron pun, and bake them in an oven.

Serve them hot with butter.

Baked Cinnamon-Sugar Pumpkin

Ingredients:
1 medium pumpkin
Butter
Sugar and cinnamon to taste

Directions:
Slice the pumpkin ¼-inch thick, peel and put a layer in the bottom of a baking dish, then a layer of sugar with a sprinkle of cinnamon and dot with butter, repeat until the pan is full. Let the top be well covered with sugar. Bake in a moderate oven until the sugar becomes like a thick syrup.

Baked Pumpkin

Ingredients:

1 medium pumpkin
Butter
Salt to taste

Directions:

Cut the pumpkin in squares and do not peel. Bake, and when soft enough, scrape it from the shells. Season with butter and salt, and serve like squash.

Calabaza en Tacha

(Courtesy of the National Honey Board)

Ingredients:

1 medium (6-10 pounds) pumpkin, seeded and cut into 8-10 large pieces
1 piloncillo cone (unrefined Mexican sugar)
1½ cups pure honey
Zest of 1 orange
Juice of 1 orange
3 cinnamon sticks
5 cloves
4 cloves allspice
2 quarts (8 cups) water
8 ounces cream cheese, at room temperature
¾ cup finely crumbled blue cheese (about 3 oz.)
½ cup finely chopped toasted walnuts
1 tablespoon minced fresh chives
2 Red Delicious apples
Salt

Directions:

In a medium stockpot combine piloncillo, pure honey, orange zest, juice of an orange, cinnamon sticks, cloves, allspice and water. Bring to a boil. Add pumpkin pieces to stockpot and simmer for approximately one hour until sauce has reduced by almost half and has become a thick syrup. The pumpkin should be fork tender, but not falling apart. Allow to cool and serve.

You can also serve it warm over non-fat yogurt and enjoy it as a fat-free dessert.

Roasted Pumpkin

Ingredients:

3 pounds sugar pumpkin
1 tablespoon grapeseed oil
Salt and pepper to taste
Pumpkin pie spices mix

You can also use the cooked pumpkin to make a purée or soup. Thin out with low-fat milk until the necessary consistency is reached. You can also use the cooked pumpkin as a base for dips or as a dessert base.

Directions:

Cut open the pumpkin, remove seeds and clean the inside with a spoon. Brush oil inside the cavity, season to taste, and place opening side down on a baking sheet. Roast for 30 to 45 minutes or until tender. Cut out and sprinkle with a little pumpkin pie spices before serving.

Desserts

Pumpkin Custard

Ingredients:

2 cups pumpkin, sieved
1 cup soft bread crumbs
2 eggs, separated
1½ cups milk
1 cup sugar
3 tablespoons butter, melted
¼ teaspoon salt
1 teaspoon orange flavoring

Directions:

Combine ingredients except egg whites in the order listed and mix well after each addition. Pour into baking dish or custard cups. Bake in a slow oven (325°F) until mixture thickens and browns. Beat the egg whites, adding 2 tablespoons of sugar, until stiff, spread on top of custard and brown lightly.

West Indies Cookies

Ingredients:
Pumpkin, grated
1 cup sugar
Butter
Cinnamon
Cornmeal (enough to bind dough together)

Directions:
Grate a piece of pumpkin, add a piece of butter (size of an egg),
a little cinnamon, a cupful of sugar, and corn meal. Bake on
greased pan.

Honey Walnut Pumpkin Pie

(Courtesy of the National Honey Board)

Ingredients:

3 eggs, slightly beaten
¾ cup honey
½ teaspoon ginger
½ teaspoon nutmeg
½ teaspoon cinnamon
½ teaspoon salt
1½ cups canned pumpkin
1 cup evaporated milk
or half-and-half
1 9-inch unbaked pie shell

Honey whipped cream:
1 cup whipping cream
3 tablespoons honey
1 teaspoon vanilla

Directions:

Combine all ingredients, except pie shell. Beat or blend until smooth. Pour into shell. Bake at 425°F for 10 minutes. Reduce oven temperature to 350°F. Bake for 35 to 40 minutes or until custard is set. Cool. Just before serving, combine ⅓ cup honey, ⅓ cup chopped walnuts and ¼ teaspoon vanilla. Carefully spread over top of pie. Serve with honey sweetened whipped cream.

Honey whipped cream:

Beat whipping cream until mixture thickens; gradually add honey and beat until soft peaks form. Fold in vanilla. Makes 2 cups.

Honey Pumpkin Mousse

(Courtesy of the National Honey Board)

Ingredients:

4 eggs, separated
¾ cup honey
16 ounces fresh pumpkin puree
2 tablespoons all-purpose flour
1½ teaspoons ground cinnamon
½ teaspoon ground ginger
¼ teaspoon ground nutmeg
¼ teaspoon salt

Directions:

In top of double boiler, combine egg whites and honey. Cook over simmering water, stirring constantly, until mixture reaches 160°F; transfer mixture to a medium bowl. Using electric mixer on high speed, beat egg whites until cool and glossy peaks form; set aside. In medium saucepan, combine egg yolks, pumpkin, flour, cinnamon, ginger, nutmeg and salt. Cook over medium heat, stirring constantly, until mixture boils; remove from heat. Gently stir ¼ of beaten egg whites into pumpkin mixture; gradually fold remaining egg whites into lightened mixture. Spoon mousse into dessert glasses; cover and chill.

Pumpkin Butter

Ingredients:

2 pounds or pints dry mashed pumpkin
1 pound sugar
4 ounces butter
Flavoring either of shaved lemon rind, cloves,
nutmeg or ginger (not pulverized)

Directions:

The pumpkin must be dry, either baked or steamed. Mash it
through a strainer, mix the sugar and butter with it and the
piece of ginger bruised, or thin shaved lemon rind; let simmer
on the stove for about an hour. It becomes thick and semitrans-
parent.

Date Pumpkin Pie

Ingredients:

1 pint milk

1 cup dry steamed pumpkin, measured after being rubbed through a sieve

¾ cup seeded dates which have been ground through a food chopper

¼ cup sugar

1 tablespoon browned flour

1 egg, beaten

½ teaspoon salt

½ teaspoon powdered caraway seed (optional)

Directions:

Heat the milk, but be careful not to boil as it will curdle. Mix the remaining ingredients, then stir the hot milk into them and mix thoroughly. Bake in a crust which has a built-up edge.

Pumpkin Marmalade

Ingredients:
Yellow pumpkins
1 pound sugar per pound of pumpkin
1 orange (or lemon) per pound of pumpkin

Directions:
Take ripe yellow pumpkins, pare and cut them into large pieces.
Scrape out the seeds, weigh them and to every pound of pumpkin take a pound of sugar and an orange or lemon. Grate the
pieces of pumpkin on a coarse grater and put in the preserving
kettle with sugar, the grated orange rind and the strained juice.
Let it boil slowly, stirring frequently and skimming it well until
it forms a smooth, thick marmalade. Put it warm into small and
sterilized glass jars and seal.

Golden Ginger Cup

Ingredients:

6 pounds pumpkin
6 cups sugar
6 lemons
1 quart water
2 ounces green ginger root

Directions:

Raw pumpkin may be diced in ⅓-inch cubes or cut into balls
with French cutter. Add the ginger root and lemons sliced very
thin (remove seeds), cover with water and let stand overnight.
Simmer slowly until pumpkin is tender, testing it with a straw
or toothpick, then add the sugar and cook until the pumpkin is
clear and the liquid jells.

Pumpkin Crème Caramel

(Courtesy of John Scheepers Kitchen Garden Seeds,
www.kitchengardenseeds.com)

There is nothing better than savoring the goodness of homegrown vegetables and herbs through winter's cold, dark months. Like serving my own pesto bubbling atop warm goat cheese with crackers, or sneaking into the freezer for my choice of herbed butters, or serving my pumpkin crème caramel on Thanksgiving.

Ingredients:
1 cup sugar
1 cup heavy cream
1 cup milk
1 tablespoon vanilla paste
3 eggs
2 egg yolks
½ cup sugar
½ cup cooked pumpkin puree
Pinch of ground cloves, cinnamon and nutmeg (optional)

To make cooked pumpkin puree, select a beautiful Rouge d'Etampes, Spookacular or Long Island Cheese pumpkin. Each pound produces about one cup of puree. Cut the pumpkin in half and scoop out the seeds and fibers. Wipe the surface with a paper towel dipped in canola oil. Place the pumpkin halves on a baking sheet, fill with about an inch of water and cover with foil.

Bake in a preheated 350°F oven for 60 to 90 minutes or until the pumpkin flesh is soft and tender when pierced with a knife.

Directions:

Pour one cup of sugar into a heavy skillet. Slowly melt the sugar until it is a smooth, golden caramel. Pour the caramel into a 1½ quart soufflé dish, swirling it around to cover the bottom and 3" up the sides. Place the soufflé dish in a baking pan of cold water.

Combine the heavy cream, milk and vanilla paste in a saucepan. Heat to scalding and simmer for 8 minutes. In a large bowl, whip the eggs and egg yolks until frothy. Slowly add ½ cup sugar, blending well. Add the cooked pumpkin puree, beating until well incorporated and smooth. Add ever so small pinches of ground cloves, cinnamon and nutmeg if you like.

In steady stream, pour the hot cream mixture into the egg mixture while whisking. Pour the custard into the soufflé dish. Bake at 350°F for one hour. Let it cool. Once cool, invert the crème caramel onto a larger plate with sides to catch the delicious caramel. Serve with a dollop of freshly whipped cream sweetened with brown sugar and a hint of vanilla.

Pumpkin Patch Cake

(Courtesy of the National Honey Board)

Ingredients:

1 cup honey

1 cup vegetable oil

15 ounces fresh pumpkin puree

1 cup ripe banana, mashed

4 eggs

1 teaspoon vanilla

3 cups whole wheat flour

2 teaspoons baking powder

2 teaspoons baking soda

1 teaspoon salt

1 tablespoon cinnamon

½ teaspoon nutmeg

¼ teaspoon cloves

1 cup walnuts, coarsely chopped

1 cup seedless raisins

Directions:

Preheat oven to 350°F. In the bowl of an electric mixer, beat together honey, oil, pumpkin, banana, eggs, and vanilla until smooth. In medium bowl, stir together flour, baking powder, baking soda, salt, and spices. Add to pumpkin mixture; mix until just combined. Fold in walnuts and raisins. Pour batter into a greased and floured 10-inch tube or bundt pan. Bake 50 to 60 minutes or until cake tests done.

Pumpkin Pudding

Ingredients:
1 large pumpkin
4 ounces butter for every pound of pumpkin
Nutmeg
⅓ pint milk
4 eggs, well-beaten
Sugar to taste

Directions:
Take a large pumpkin, pare it, and remove the seeds. Cut half of
it into thin slices, and boil these gently in water until they are
quite soft, then rub them through a fine sieve with the back of
a wooden spoon. Measure the pulp, and with each pint put four
ounces of butter and a large nutmeg, grated. Stir the mixture
briskly for a minute or two, then add the third of a pint of hot
milk and four well-beaten eggs. Pour the pudding into a buttered
dish, and bake in a moderate oven for about an hour. Sugar may
be added to taste.

Velvety Pumpkin Cheesecake

(Courtesy of John Scheepers Kitchen Garden Seeds,
www.kitchengardenseeds.com)

Ingredients:

Crust:

1 teaspoon cinnamon
¼ cup sugar
¼ cup melted unsalted butter
1½ cups crushed ginger snap cookies

Filling:

1 pound cream cheese (at room temperature)
1 pound ricotta cheese

1 cup sour cream
1 cup cooked, pureed pumpkin flesh
3 eggs
1 cup sugar
2 teaspoons vanilla
3 tablespoons cornstarch
Pinch of salt

Note: You can vary the degree of pumpkin flavor: the total contribution of the pumpkin and sour cream should be two cups however you divide it.

Directions:

Crust:

Preheat oven to 350°F. Mix crust ingredients together and spread in bottom of a 10" greased springform cake pan.

Filling:

In large mixing bowl, beat the cream cheese until smooth. Add the eggs, one at a time, beating until smooth. Add sugar slowly and mix until fluffy. Add ricotta cheese, sour cream and pureed pumpkin and mix until smooth. Add vanilla, cornstarch and salt and mix to blend.

Pour mixture over crust. Bake at 350°F for one hour. Turn oven off and leave cheesecake in closed oven for another hour. Remove from oven and let cool to room temperature. Refrigerate. Remove from springform pan. Lovely with freshly whipped cream sweetened with a bit of brown sugar.

Pumpkin Harvest Bread with Ice Cream

Ingredients:

1½ cups flour
½ cup cornmeal
1½ teaspoons baking powder
1 teaspoon baking soda
¼ teaspoon salt
2 teaspoons ground cinnamon
½ teaspoon ground nutmeg
1 cup solid pack cooked pumpkin

2 eggs
1 cup packed brown sugar
¼ cup vegetable oil
¼ cup apricot preserves
½ cup raisins
½ cup walnuts
4 cups low-fat vanilla ice cream

Directions:

Preheat the oven to 350°F.

Combine the flour, cornmeal, baking powder, baking soda, salt, cinnamon, and nutmeg in a bowl. Beat the pumpkin, eggs, brown sugar, oil and preserves in a large mixing bowl. Incorporate the flour mixture and blend until well mixed. Stir in the raisins, walnuts, and transfer to a greased and floured loaf pan. Bake for 50 to 55 minutes or until wooden pick inserted into the center comes out clean. Cool in pan for 5 to 10 minutes. Transfer the loaf to a wire rack and cool completely before slicing. Serve each slice with ¼ cup low-fat vanilla ice cream.

Pumpkin Cookies

(Contributed by Chef Nancy Berkoff, The Vegetarian Resource Group, Vegetarian Journal, www.vrg.org)

Ingredients:

Vegetable oil spray
1 cup non-hydrogenated vegan margarine
1 cup sugar (use your favorite vegan variety)
1 cup canned or cooked pumpkin
3 tablespoons mashed banana
1 teaspoon vanilla extract
2 cups unbleached flour
1 teaspoon baking powder
1 teaspoon cinnamon
1 teaspoon ground ginger
½ teaspoon cloves
½ teaspoon allspice
½ cup chopped raisins
½ cup chopped dates

Note: Do not overbake these cookies, as they can be rather dry. These go well with hot or cold tea, milk, or coffee. The cookies can also be crumbled over cooked hot cereal.

Directions:

Preheat oven to 375°F. Spray a baking sheet with oil.

In a large bowl, combine margarine and sugar until well mixed. Add pumpkin, banana, and vanilla and stir to combine. In a separate bowl, mix together the flour, baking powder, and spices. Add to pumpkin mixture and stir. Mix in raisins and dates. Drop by teaspoonfuls onto the baking sheet. Bake cookies for 15 minutes or until just crisp on the edges. Makes approximately 48 cookies.

Eggless Pumpkin Custard

(Contributed by Chef Nancy Berkoff, The Vegetarian Resource
Group, Vegetarian Journal, www.vrg.org)

Ingredients:

2 cups canned pumpkin (not spiced or sweetened)
1½ cups silken tofu
1 cup soy or almond milk
4 tablespoons sugar (use your favorite vegan variety)
1 tablespoon maple syrup
2 teaspoons cinnamon
1 teaspoon cloves
1 teaspoon nutmeg
½ teaspoon orange zest

Directions:

Preheat oven to 375°F.

Combine pumpkin, tofu, and milk in a blender or food processor
and blend until smooth. Add remaining ingredients and mix well
to combine.

Pour into individual custard cups or a baking dish and bake for
20 minutes or until custard is set. Serves 8.

Resources

Finding Local Farms, Farmstands, and Sustainable Food Organizations

Local Harvest

www.localharvest.org
Use the search tool provided by the Local Harvest website to find farmers' markets, co-ops, farms, and other sustainable food sources in your local area.

Eat Well Guide

www.eatwellguide.org
The Eat Well Guide offers a comprehensive search of local organizations, farms, farmers markets, restaurants, and co-ops that offer local, organic, and sustainable food.

Local.com

www.local.com
Search for local fruit and vegetables stands, farms, organizations and more on this website.

Pumpkin Patches and More

www.pumpkinpatchesandmore.org
Check out the state and regional directory made available by Pumpkin Patches and More to find pumpkin patches and farms near you. The website also lists information about various pumpkin festivals, events, and county and state pumpkin fairs.

State, Regional, and National Pumpkin Growers Associations and Groups

Central Wisconsin Pumpkin Growers

www.cwpg.org

Connecticut Giant Squash and Pumpkin Growers Association
www.ctpumpkin.com

Illinois Giant Pumpkin Growers Association
www.igpga.org

Indiana Pumpkin Growers Association
www.ipga.us

Maine Pumpkin Growers Organization
www.mainepumpkins.com

New Hampshire Giant Pumpkin Growers Association
www.nhgpga.org

New York State Giant Pumpkin Growers Association
www.nysgpga.com

Ohio Valley Giant Pumpkin Growers
www.ovgpg.com

Pacific Giant Vegetable Growers
www.pgvg.org

Pacific Northwest Giant Pumpkin Growers
www.pnwgpg.com

Pennsylvania Giant Pumpkin Growers Association
www.pgpga.com

Rocky Mountain Giant Vegetable Growers
www.coloradopumpkins.com

Southern Ohio Giant Pumpkin Growers
www.sogpg.com

United Fresh Produce Association
www.unitedfresh.org

Utah Giant Pumpkin Growers
www.utahpumpkingrowers.com

Vermont Giant Vegetable Growers Association
http://vermontgiants.tripod.com

Acknowledgments

Hatherleigh Press would like to extend a special thank you to Jo Brielyn and Christina Anger–without your hard work and creativity this book would not have been possible.

My Recipes

My Recipes

My Recipes

_____

_____

_____

_____

_____

_____

_____

_____

_____

_____

_____

_____

_____

_____

_____

_____

_____

_____

_____

_____

_____

My Recipes

My Recipes

My Recipes

My Recipes